READY, SET, WRITE YOUR BOOK

A 21-STEP GUIDE TO ASSIST WITH WRITING YOUR BOOK

DR. SYNOVIA DOVER-HARRIS

Ready, Set, Write Your Book. A 21-step guide to assist with writing your book

First Printing
ISBN 978-1-943284-16-0 (pbk.)
ISBN 978-1-943284-17-7 (ebk)

A2Z Books, LLC
Lithonia, GA 30058
www.A2ZBooksPublishing.com
Manufactured in the United States of America
A2Z Books Publishing has allowed this work to remain exactly as the author intended, verbatim.

INTRODUCTION

If you have this book, you fall under one of the three categories:

1. The person who has always wanted to write a book.
2. The person who has started a book, but cannot finish it.
3. The person who never thought about writing a book, but is curious about the process.

When I wrote my first book over 10 years ago, I did not know how much of an effect it would have on other individuals, as well as myself. I would hear people say; wow, you wrote a book, and the next thing I would hear is; I have always wanted to write a book. Over the years, what I also learned is that most people think it is a hard and daunting task that is impossible to do, but with the right techniques, motivation, time, and organization anyone can write a book.

Whether it is a self-help book, a steamy love novel, a crime-filled fiction book, or even a cookbook, I believe that everyone has a story to tell.

This Ready Set Write your book, book is 21 strategies that will assist you with the beginning, middle, and end processes of book writing and publishing a book.

This book was created to:
- Educate the current author.
- Guide the aspiring author.
- Motivate the not sure author.

HOW TO USE THIS GUIDE

This guide contains 21 Steps to assist with writing your book. All of the steps are action items that you will need to complete and will assist you with starting and completing the book writing process. This book can be utilized to write any kind of book. Most of the steps should be easy to complete and implement. However, because this is a resource guide, assistance may be required.

You will need:

- An allocated place to work and write.
- At least 30-45 minutes to complete each step (some may require more, and others may require less).
- A computer or cell phone (to conduct research).
- Something to write on (notebook/journal).
- Something to write with (pen/pencil).
- A calendar or scheduling system of some sort to create timelines/deadlines.

The steps/action items are strategically designed to align and propel you in the right direction to write your book..

READY...

SET...

WRITE YOUR BOOK!

CONTENTS

Step 1
Purpose

Step 1 is identifying your purpose or reason for writing a book. Identifying your purpose for writing is important because to know where you are going, you need to know why you are going there. Your purpose will be your inspiration to start the book, but the motivation to complete the book. You need to decide what are you trying to say and whom are you trying to say it to.

Most people write books because they have a message they want to share. While others write to inform. Some people write to provide knowledge and others write to heal themselves. Some people write to build brands and obtain credibility, and others write a book because it is just something they have always wanted to do.

Are you writing a book?
- ✓ To Entertain?
- ✓ To Educate?
- ✓ To Encourage?
- ✓ To Enlighten?
- ✓ To Express?

Now ask yourself who you are.
- ✓ Are you writing a book because you have a compelling story you want to share?
- ✓ Are you writing a book because you want to make money?
- ✓ Are you writing a book because you want to build your brand?

Take the next 30 minutes and identify your purpose for writing a Book…

USE THIS AREA TO WRITE
ABOUT YOUR BOOK

_____

_____

_____

_____

_____

_____

_____

_____

_____

_____

_____

_____

_____

_____

_____

_____

_____

_____

_____

_____

_____

_____

_____

_____

Step 2
Category

Step 2 is deciding on a book category. There are many genres, but there are only two definite book categories; which is either a fiction book or a non-fiction book.

- A fiction book is based on imaginary things, people, & places.
- A non-fiction book is based on facts, true events, people, & places.

In simpler form:

- A fiction book is not true and is to entertain.
- A non-fiction book is true and is to inform.

Non-fiction writers need to:

- ✓ Have a firm grasp of the English language.
- ✓ Be able to write things that are clear and effective.
- ✓ Be a good researcher.
- ✓ Be strong.
- ✓ Be self-disciplined.

A fiction writer needs to:

- ✓ Be original.
- ✓ Be innovative.
- ✓ Be passionate.
- ✓ Be disciplined.
- ✓ Tell a story in a way that is entertaining.

A non-fiction book is The A2Z of Success by Synovia Dover-Harris.
A fiction book is Harry Potter by J.K. Rowling.

Take the next 30 minutes and research book categories and identify what category of book you will be writing …

USE THIS AREA TO WRITE
ABOUT YOUR BOOK

_____

_____

_____

_____

_____

_____

_____

_____

_____

_____

_____

_____

_____

_____

Step 3
Book Genres

Step 3 is choosing a book genre. A genre is a literary term used to define a group of works with similar characteristics such as characters, themes, and setting. A book genre is a class in which the book will be written under the non-fiction or fiction category

5 top non-fiction genres are:
1. Self-Help
2. Religion/Spirituality
3. Memoirs & Narratives
4. Business/Finance
5. Health/Fitness

5 top fiction genres are:
1. Young Adult
2. Fantasy
3. Literary Fiction
4. Children's Books
5. Science Fiction

Choosing a genre should be based on what you are writing and whom you are writing for. Who is your target audience and what are you trying to say to them and why? Research the type of book you want to write based on your purpose and choose a genre. Additionally, if you have already started writing or want to write your book/story first, your book/story will choose the genre.

Take the next 30 minutes and research book genre and identify what genre of book you will be writing ...

USE THIS AREA TO WRITE
ABOUT YOUR BOOK

_____

_____

_____

_____

_____

_____

_____

_____

_____

_____

_____

_____

_____

Step 4
Book Audience

Step 4 is identifying your book audience or your target market. Now that you have a category and a genre, it is now time to figure out who is your audience. The biggest mistake new authors make is thinking their book is for everyone and not having a specific target audience. Rule #1: No book is for everyone. Your Book Audience/Target Market should be based on what you are saying. Your audience needs to be known before you begin the book writing process so that you will know how to communicate with them effectively.

For example: If you are writing a non-fiction self-help book on starting a business, you will need to know if the book will be written for young, educated, professionals or kids. You will want to know if your target audience lives in the south or are retirees looking to start a business. You will write as if you are speaking directly to them.

Knowing your audience will assist with determining:
- ✓ The topics
- ✓ The word usage
- ✓ The storyline
- ✓ The book cover
- ✓ The marketing

Determine your audience with the following demographics:
- ✓ Class
- ✓ Education
- ✓ Gender
- ✓ Age
- ✓ Income
- ✓ Etc.

Take the next 30 minutes, research book audience/target market, and identify whom you are writing this book for …

USE THIS AREA TO WRITE
ABOUT YOUR BOOK

_____

_____

_____

_____

_____

_____

_____

_____

_____

_____

_____

_____

_____

_____

_____

Step 5
Book Title

Step 5 is creating a book title. Titles are the most important component of your book and are actually more important than the cover. Book titles determine if a potential reader will read your book. If someone is talking about your book and cannot see the cover, they will hear the title and instantly become intrigued or turned off.

If a title is good, the potential reader will become interested and will more than likely look more into the book.

When choosing a book title, you want to make sure:
- ✓ It's catchy
- ✓ It's appealing to your target audience
- ✓ It's not too long, but also not too short
- ✓ It's easy to say
- ✓ It's easy to remember

The top ten book titles of all time:
1. Do Androids Dream of Electric Sheep - By Philip K Dick
2. Everything I Never Told You - By Celest Ng
3. Is Everyone Hanging Out Without Me? (and Other Concerns) - By Mindy Kaling
4. The Electric Kool-Aid Acid Test - By Tom Wolfe
5. Are You There, Vodka? It's Me, Chelsea - By Chelsea Handler
6. The Devil Wears Prada - By Lauren Weisberger
7. The Curious Incident of the Dog in the Night-Time - By Mark Haddon
8. How to Win Friends and Influence People -By Dale Carnegie
9. Cloudy with a Chance of Meatballs - By Judi Barrett
10. Love in the Time of Cholera - By Gabriel García Márquez

Take the next 60 minutes and research book titles and create one for your book ...

USE THIS AREA TO WRITE

ABOUT YOUR BOOK

_____

_____

_____

_____

_____

_____

_____

_____

_____

_____

_____

Step 6
Book Topics

Step 6 is determining your book topics/chapter titles or book content. Now that you know your book's purpose, category, genre, and audience, we can now determine what your book topics or content will be.

You may have a lot of ideas going through your head, which can be overwhelming. However, by organizing your thoughts and writing down the actual topics you want to cover in your book will help you out tremendously.

You can choose a book topic based on:
- ✓ Something you are passionate about.
- ✓ Something you do not know much about, but is in high demand.
- ✓ Something you are knowledgeable in.

You can choose your chapter titles by breaking down the topic into smaller topics. For example:
- ✓ Management can be broken down to:
  - o Communication
  - o Professionalism
  - o Attitude
  - o Etc.

If you choose a topic that you do not know much about but is in high demand, you have to conduct the research, but this book may have a great earning potential and thus giving you a passion for writing. Additionally, if you chose to write a book on a topic you are knowledgeable about, there is also great earning potential, and you should enjoy the writing process.

Take the next 60 minutes and research book topics based on your interest and create chapter titles (you will use for an outline later) ...

USE THIS AREA TO WRITE
ABOUT YOUR BOOK

_____

_____

_____

_____

_____

_____

_____

_____

_____

_____

_____

_____

_____

_____

Step 7
Research

Step 7 is conducting research. Now that you have a book concept, it is now time to carry out some research on your chosen topic. You do not want to write a book that no one wants to read, so, before you begin the writing process, do your due diligence and see what's out there already that is written on your subject and see how you can put a twist on that to make your book more promotable.

Research for a non-fiction book can be:
- ✓ Already published books on that particular concept.
- ✓ Published articles on the concept.
- ✓ Blogs
- ✓ Field Study (Conducting interviews on actual topic).

Research for a fiction book can be:
- ✓ Visiting/Traveling to locations that are like the setting of your book.
- ✓ Interviewing individuals with the personality traits of your characters.
- ✓ Visiting the library.
- ✓ Field study (interviewing storyline).

Document information you find and use this data to assist with writing your book.

Take the next 60 minutes and conduct some research …

USE THIS AREA TO WRITE
ABOUT YOUR BOOK

_____

_____

_____

_____

_____

_____

_____

_____

_____

_____

_____

_____

_____

_____

Step 8
Who is Writing?

Step 8 is identifying who is writing the book. You know that you want to write a book, you have your topics, title, and have done the research, which means your foundation is built, but now you have to decide how the book will be written.

Answer the following questions:
- ✓ Will you write alone?
- ✓ Will you hire a ghostwriter?
- ✓ Will you have a coauthor?

Writing alone, hiring a ghostwriter, and working with another writer all has its advantages and disadvantages.
- ✓ The advantage of writing alone is you are on your own time, the information will be relayed exactly how you want it, and the disadvantage of writing alone is no accountability partner and limited resources because two heads working on one project is better than one.
- ✓ The advantages of enlisting a coauthor are the work is shared and you will have access to more information, and the disadvantage is the coauthor has to agree on decisions and you have time constraints because you are working on someone else's time.
- ✓ The advantage of hiring a ghostwriter is having someone else do the work, which gives you more time to promote, but the disadvantages are the cost and not knowing if the story written will actually be in your voice.

You have to weigh each option and choose which one is right for you and your project.

Take the next 20 minutes and decide how the book will be written ...

USE THIS AREA TO WRITE
ABOUT YOUR BOOK

Step 9
Book Length

Step 9 is determining the length of your book. This step is vital. If you are writing alone, this will be decided alone, but if you are hiring a ghostwriter or working with a coauthor, you can decide this together. The length of your book is very important because it will determine how much time you need to allocate to get the book completed.

Research indicates that a novel should be between 80,000 and 89,999 words. Research also suggests that a nonfiction book should be at least 50,000 words; however, there are really no rules, because some novels are short stories and there have been bestselling nonfiction books that were only 3000 words long.

My first book was only 50 pages long and a little over 5000 words. I made it only 50 pages because my target audience was small business owners who did not have a lot of time to read a book nor did they want to have to go through a lot of pages to find the marketing information they needed. Additionally, I have a friend whose book was over 400 pages, and although it was an excellent book, I discovered that most people that purchased her book never finished reading the book, because it was too long.

Therefore, you want to:

- Analyze your target audience and chosen topic and determine how much information you should be able to put inside a book.
- Go to the Library and Bookstore and see what you like.

If you find yourself with a lot of information, you can always write a second or third book and make it a series, and once you are writing, you can always add or deduct pages or word count.

Take the next 60 minutes and look at books you have around the house or go to a bookstore and determine what length of book you want to write ...

USE THIS AREA TO WRITE
ABOUT YOUR BOOK

Step 10
Set Writing Goals

Step 10 is creating writing goals. To get to your desired word or page count, and publishing deadline, you have to set writing goals. Even if you set 250-words a day or 2 pages day, specific goals need to be set. These goals will keep you on track and keep you motivated and inspired.

The smaller the goal, the easier to accomplish, but the bigger the goal, the faster you will reach to the finish line. However, if the goals are too big, you may get discouraged and not write at all.

Writing goals can be set for the day, the week, the month, or the year but make sure that they are SMART Goals, which are Specific, Measurable, Attainable, Relevant, & Time-Bound.

For example:
- ✓ *Specific* is who, what, when, where and why.
  For example: I want to write a 50-page book by July 30.
- ✓ *Measurable* is the metrics for the goal you are trying to achieve. 50 pages are the amount that has to be written.
- ✓ *Achievable* is having the ability to achieve this goal, by being motivated and having time and resources in place to achieve.
- ✓ *Relevant* is the significance of achieving the goal. For example: I want to achieve this goal of writing the 50-page book because it is needed for the workshop I am teaching in September.
- ✓ *Time Bound* is the time the goal requires to be completed. For Example: If today is June 1st, then writing 1 page a day for 50 days is achievable because there are 60 days available. However, if it is July 1st, there is still time to write the 50 pages by July 30th, but more will have to be written, and the goals will need to be set based on the time available to achieve the goal.

Take the next 45 minutes and Set Your Writing Goals ...

USE THIS AREA TO WRITE
ABOUT YOUR BOOK

Step 11
Where will you write?

Step 11 is deciding where you will write. If you decided not to enlist a ghostwriter, the only way to get the book done is to sit down and write it. One of the main issues I have heard from my authors over the years is not having a dedicated place or places to write. A schedule is good, but not effective if you do not have a place to write. Having a location for writing your book is so very important because where you write can determine what you write.

The content, as well as the quality of your story is contingent upon where you are writing. Some authors like myself need complete isolation and quietness when they write. Whereas, other authors like noise and many things going on in the background to get their books finished.

- ✓ If you have young kids like myself, I cannot concentrate if they are talking. Therefore, I turn the T.V. off, close my door and write.

- ✓ I have an author who cannot write at home at all. She likes going to coffee shops or bookstores.

- ✓ I know another author who writes in her office at work. She said when she is at home, she is not inspired, and when she is at a place like a coffee shop, she gets distracted. Therefore, writing at work is the best place for her.

Your writing environment is important, but the truth of the matter is, you will not know what works for you until you have tried a few places and see how and where the juices flow.

Take the next few days and test where you write bests. Go to a bookstore, coffee shop, try writing at home, and you can even try writing at work, at a park, or in your backyard …

USE THIS AREA TO WRITE
ABOUT YOUR BOOK

_____

_____

_____

_____

_____

_____

_____

_____

_____

_____

_____

_____

_____

_____

_____

_____

_____

_____

_____

_____

_____

_____

_____

_____

_____

_____

Step 12
How will you write?

Step 12 is deciding how you will write. If you decided against a ghostwriter and you will be writing on your own, the next decision to make is how you will write. Will you pick up a piece of paper and start writing the old school way, or will you do it the way I do it; which is by typing it? There are also voice recognition software and programs now available where you talk and the software transcribes your information, which is talking and the program writes what you have said.

There are advantages and disadvantages of each.

- ✓ If you manually write your book, eventually your book will have to be typed. Manually writing can be easy if you are not a computer person, but I have seen firsthand where content was mistyped because the actual author did not type the information. Human error is always possible.
- ✓ If you use a transcribing software, which is probably the easiest of the three, you would just need to choose the correct program to fit your needs and just as a person can type information wrong, you run the chance of the software doing the same thing because the program will not know the difference between "for" or "four" or "two or "to" or "too" Therefore, the document would still need to be edited to ensure proper grammar is being utilized.
- ✓ If you decide to type your book yourself, which is how it is done mostly your words will not be changed and what you want to say will be said.

Weigh your options, look at your time frame, and decide how your book will be written.

Take the next 30 minutes and decide how your book will be written ...

Step 13
Book Writing Schedule

Step 13 is creating your writing schedule. Now that you have a book topic, a book length, your writing goals, and where you will write, you need to create a writing schedule.

Creating a writing schedule is very important because you want to actually complete your book. A writing schedule will keep you organized and motivated, as well as let everyone including yourself know that you are committed to completing your book.

Starting a book is easy, but completing a book is very difficult. I know firsthand because personally, I have six incomplete books. I also have authors and a host of friends who have started writing books but have not been able to complete them.

The #1 reason for incomplete books is the lack of time.

Ask yourself; how much time can I realistically dedicate to writing and completing my book?

Next: ask yourself; when do I want my book complete?

Your goals and the amount of pages/words chosen will determine how often and how much you need to write.

For example: If you wanted to produce 80 pages in 4 weeks, you would have to write 10 pages each week or per 7 days, which is 1.42 pages a day. If you want to produce 120 pages in 6 weeks, you would have to write a minimum of 20 pages per week or 2.85 pages a day.

Now ask yourself; will I write in the mornings, during lunch, in the evenings, after everyone is in bed, or will I be a weekend writer? You have to determine your writing schedule based on your lifestyle and how much you want to be written and in what time period.

Take the next 60 minutes and create a writing schedule …

Schedule Example:

Mondays:

6:00–6:30 am: Wake up 30 minutes early; write 250 words or 1 page

12:00–12:30 pm: Take half of lunch to write 250 words or 1 page

7:00–8:00 pm: Set aside a full hour for writing after dinner; Write 500 words or 2 pages

Tuesdays:

6:00–6:30 am: Wake up 30 minutes early; write 250 words or 1 page.

12:00–12:30 pm: Take half of lunch to write; 250 words or 1 page.

8:30–11:00 pm: Continue writing after coming home from work; write 1000 words

Wednesdays:

12:00–12:30 pm: Take half of lunch to write 500 words

7:00–11:00 pm: Take the night off after dinner to write 1500+ words or 5 to 10 pages.

Thursdays:

6:00–6:30 am: Wake up 30 minutes early; write 500 words

7:30–8:30 pm: Attempt to get 500–1000 words written

10:00–11:00 pm: Finish up daily writing goal before bed; 500–1000 words, or until daily word count of is reached

Fridays:

6:00–6:30 am: Wake up 30 minutes early; write 500 words

12:00–12:30 pm: Take half of lunch to write 500 words

10:00 pm–12:30 am: Stay up late to write; squeeze out 1000+ words

Saturdays-Writing Break

Sundays-Writing Break

With this schedule, you would write approximately 8000 words.

Note: This is only a scheduling example and is not the schedule you have to use.

Writing Tip: Always add your style and your voice to your writing.

USE THIS AREA TO WRITE
ABOUT YOUR BOOK

_____

_____

_____

_____

_____

_____

_____

_____

_____

_____

_____

_____

_____

_____

Step 14
Book Writing Outline

Step 14 is creating a book outline. The purpose of creating a book outline is to organize your ideas. So think of it as a blueprint that will show you what goes where.

Creating a Book Outline helps:
- ✓ Eliminate writer's block and complete the book quickly because you already know what you are writing about, and you know what is coming next.

Creating an outline also:
- ✓ Allows you to solve problems faster.
- ✓ Make changes in the storyline or plot if needed.

Creating an outline is necessary for both nonfiction and fiction books.

- ✓ Outlining for a fiction book can be completed through Walk The Line, A Wall Grid, The Snow Flake Method, Mind Mapping, or a Basic Document where you can write the key plot and the action, the characters, and the theme (etc.) on a computer, a sheet of paper, and even index cards. Additionally, you could use one or a number of these to get to your storyline and chapter outlines.
- ✓ Outlining for a nonfiction book can be completed by choosing your Topic, then choosing Sub-Topics, which will be chapters, then chose sub topics of sub topics, which are the minor points of the major points.

For example: Topic is Management- Sub-Topics is Communication, Professionalism, Vision, Motivation, & Problem Solving. Then, subtopics are broken down even further.
Note: These outlines can be changed as needed.

Take the next 60 minutes and create a book outline …

USE THIS AREA TO WRITE
ABOUT YOUR BOOK

_____

_____

_____

_____

_____

_____

_____

_____

_____

_____

_____

_____

_____

Step 15
Book Writing Process

Step 15 is creating a book writing process. A book writing process is different from an outline. An outline lets you know what you are going to write and the process is the system in which you will write.

Despite the category or genre, every writer needs a process. The basic and easiest writing process is:

- ✓ **Prewriting**, which is brainstorming and organizing ideas as well as writing without a filter. This is where all the ideas from the outline will be written.
- ✓ **Draft/Writing** is the next step, which is writing the outline and the ideas in its first book form or storytelling method. This is to organize the story, define word choices, and write.
- ✓ **Revision** is the next step, which you will take the writings, read it, and make necessary changes while reading what was previously written. The revision step can last a few rounds but is to clarify, reorganize, and refine.
- ✓ **Editing** is the next step. Although it is always and highly recommended to enlist the help of a professional editor, the writer should always make the first edits. In this step, you will check for grammar, punctuation, sentence, and word usage and ensure that what is written is what you are trying to relay.
- ✓ **Publishing** is the final step of the book writing process. This is where you will decide how your book will be presented to the world.

Take the next 45 minutes and research book writing processes and create your book writing process …

USE THIS AREA TO WRITE
ABOUT YOUR BOOK

Step 16
Dedicated Reading Time

Step 16 is dedicated reading time. Although this is not a part of actually writing, reading helps with writing because good readers make good writers. It might sound cliché, but it is in fact true. Active readers have a more diverse vocabulary and have better writing styles and skills. Therefore, having dedicated time to read will be beneficial to you completing your book.

You may or may not be an avid reader and studies show that only 27% of Americans are readers in the first place, but now that you are on your way to becoming a bestselling author yourself, you need to read more.

It is not necessary to read books on the topic or genre in which you are writing, but reading can:
- ✓ Open your mind and make you a more critical thinker.
- ✓ Create innovative thoughts, which makes better storylines and a book that is more entertaining.
- ✓ Put you at ease and reduce stress to be able to complete projects in general.
- ✓ Restart your brain to write if you have writer's block.

Active readers are happier people and are known to be the best writers and authors.

30 minutes a day is all that is needed. My recommendation is to put together a list of books that you have either already started and have not finished or books that you have always wanted to read. Pick them up or order online and get to reading.

Take the next 30 minutes and create your dedicated reading time and reading list …

USE THIS AREA TO WRITE
ABOUT YOUR BOOK

Step 17
Editing

Step 17 is editing. It does not matter how good of a writer you are, every book needs to be edited.

Editing is preparing your book to become published.

An unedited book will affect your book sales. As a publisher and author myself, I have spent lots of time and money on editing, and it has always been worth the time and money spent.

Editing your book can:
- ✓ Remove unnecessary verbiage.
- ✓ Give you a more professional book.

You never want a book that is so full of mistakes that it is overly distracting and turns off the reader. Unbelievably, I found a mistake in one of Barack Obama's books when he first became president, but it was something minor.

Because, editing is usually completed by a human, there is still always room for error, however a mistake here and there is not a problem, but when reading a book and the mistakes take precedence over the content or book concept, this is not professional. If your book is hard to follow and understand, your readers might get annoyed and upset. You never gets a second chance to make a first impression, and you might lose that reader for life. I have personally found that some authors do not like going through the editing route because it takes a lot of time and can sometimes be expensive. However, editing is always recommended.

You can hire an editor to correct grammar and spelling, ensure the book is flowing correctly and to make sure what you are saying actually make sense. There are editors you can find on Google and the company Fiverr that are inexpensive. You can also go to a local university or ask around.

Take the next 30 minutes and research editors...

USE THIS AREA TO WRITE
ABOUT YOUR BOOK

Step 18
Book Cover

Step 18 is deciding on a book cover design. Never judge a book by its cover is one of the oldest sayings, but in the case of an actual book, this is not the case. Your book will be judged by its title and next the cover. Your book cover is the face of your book and what will be seen before the book is ever opened. There are millions of books published a year so what will separate your book from the rest, is the title and the cover.

If you decide to self-publish without going through a self-publishing company, you will have to get your cover designed on your own, which can be done by hiring someone or designing it yourself with the many software available. Additionally, if you publish with a traditional publisher, most of them have a graphic artist of some sort that will provide you with a book cover. You can give them an idea of what you want and their designers will create a design for you.

Make sure your Cover Design is:
- ✓ Professional
- ✓ Innovative
- ✓ Appealing
- ✓ Represents the Content of the Book
- ✓ Have a Meaning
- ✓ Simple, yet Strong

If you are confused and do not know what you want your cover to look like, do some research. You can look on Amazon, go to a bookstore, or visit your local library. You will definitely find interest and inspiration there. Make sure you write down the colors, fonts, themes, and book cover titles that you like, so you can refer back to it later when getting your cover designed.

Take the next few days and research cover designs and create a mockup of what you think you want your cover to look like …

USE THIS AREA TO WRITE
ABOUT YOUR BOOK

_____

_____

_____

_____

_____

_____

_____

_____

_____

_____

_____

_____

_____

Step 19
Copyrighting

Step 19 is copyrighting. Your book needs to be copyrighted, but I bet you did not know that whenever you write a story, a book or even a paper for school, you automatically own the copyrights to it. Whenever you create something original and it is set up in a way that someone else can experience it, your work is under copyright protection from the moment it is created.

Copyright is a form of protection given to the authors or creators of "original works of authorship," including literary, dramatic, musical, artistic and other intellectual works.

Copyright allows you to:

- ✓ Create duplicates of your work
- ✓ Issue copies of your work
- ✓ Perform your work publicly (such as for plays, film, dances or music)
- ✓ Display your work publicly
- ✓ Make "derivative works" (including making modifications, adaptations or other new uses of work, or translating the work to another media).

Although your work is automatically copyrighted when completed, if you want to, you can obtain legal paperwork at www.copyright.gov for a small fee. Additionally, if you collaborate with a publisher, they can file your copyright for you.

Note: Copyright does not protect facts, ideas, systems, or methods of operation. However, it will protect a book or operating manual that explains these ideas, systems or methods.

Take the next 30 minutes and research copyrights and decide how you will copyright your book …

USE THIS AREA TO WRITE
ABOUT YOUR BOOK

Step 20
Publishing

Step 20 is deciding how to publish. The whole point of writing your book in the first place is to get it published and in the hands of the readers. You have the option of self-publishing, working with a literary agent to assist with landing a traditional publishing contract, and you have the possibility of working with a self-publishing company that works like a traditional publisher, but you pay to publish.

Each publishing option has its pros and cons.

A few advantages of self-publishing are:
- ✓ Control, because you get to decide what it looks like, how it is marketed etc.
- ✓ Money, because you get to keep most of it because you are the publisher and do not have to pay traditional publishing fees.
- ✓ Time, because you are working on your schedule and put the book out as fast or take as long as you like.

A few disadvantages of self-publishing are:
- ✓ Not knowing what you are doing (although there are many resources to help).
- ✓ Not looking professional, because editing, cover designs, and everything that a traditional publisher has perfected are new to the self-publishers.

If you decide to go the traditional publishing route, obtaining a literary agent is required and can be a long, tedious process. However, if that is the route you decide to go, the advantages are; you get all the help you need.

Take the next 60 minutes and research publishing options and decide how you will publish your book ...

USE THIS AREA TO WRITE
ABOUT YOUR BOOK

Step 21
Marketing

Step 21 is creating a marketing strategy. Marketing is mandatory once your book is published. With the many platforms and the ease of writing and publishing books, there is something like 1 million books published per year worldwide. In order for you and your book to not get lost in that number, you have to create a marketing strategy to get your book in front of your target audience.

Creating a book marketing strategy is crucial and may sound difficult, but it is not. Positioning is the key, and this is where you will create the brand for your book, which will make it stand out from other books. The title, the topic, the quality & the cover design is the position, and the marketing will be based on your position. For example: If you wrote a book called the 10-minute mommy makeover guide, you would want to make sure the cover is designed in a way that would appeal to moms, and it could be marketed at OB GYN's office, Pediatrician offices and in mommy groups on Social Media, etc.

Here are a few tips to market your book:
- ✓ Have a Book Launch.
- ✓ Create a website/ Blog about book or topic.
- ✓ Collaborate with likes platforms.
- ✓ Create Social Media Group and Business Pages.
- ✓ Speak free on the book's topic.
- ✓ Create a workshop, class, or other services on topic.
- ✓ Give away free chapters to get people interested.
- ✓ Create a Tripwire to gain customers.
- ✓ Build an Email List
- ✓ Use #Hashtags
- ✓ Brand-t-shirts, pens, mugs, etc.

Take the next 60 minutes and decide how you will market your book once ready to publish ...

USE THIS AREA TO WRITE
ABOUT YOUR BOOK

Letter from the Author:

Congratulations on completing this 21 step guide to assist with writing your book. I commend you for making the first steps and working diligently to getting to this point. As an author of numerous books, I know that a strong foundation is needed to start and complete a book. Many people think that writing a book is impossible to do, but I know that with these 21 steps, the process can be easier. Completing this book and all the necessary steps is just the beginning of your book writing and publishing journey. I want you to use this guide as a resource even after you have completed your 21 steps. Always remember that everyone has a story to tell and the world is just waiting for yours.

Thanks,
Dr. Synovia Dover-Harris

Contact Info
Dr.Synovia@A2ZBookspublishing.com
Facebook/Synovia Dover-Harris
Instagram @Dr.Synovia

Order online at amazon.com and all other online distributors

Also Available:

Ready Set Build your brand
Ready Set Launch your business

Coming Soon:
Ready Set Launch your Private Label
Ready Set Build your Team

DR. SYNOVIA DOVER HARRIS

Interested in Writing and or Publishing a BOOK???

Visit: www.A2ZBooksPublishing.com

www.ingramcontent.com/pod-product-compliance
Lightning Source LLC
Chambersburg PA
CBHW031904200326
41597CB00012B/534